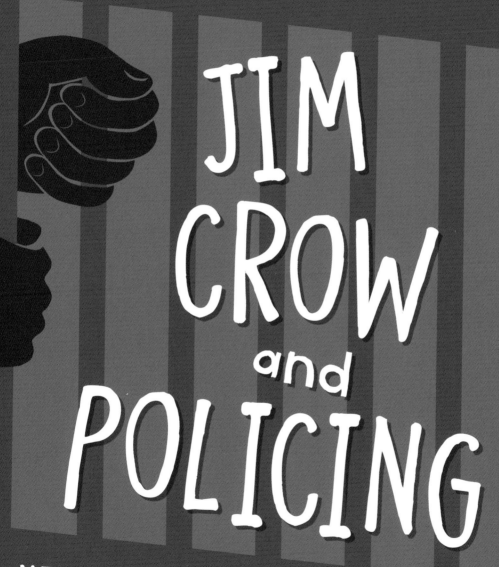

RACIAL JUSTICE IN AMERICA
HISTORIES

JIM CROW and POLICING

KEVIN P. WINN WITH KELISA WING

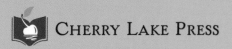

CHERRY LAKE PRESS

Published in the United States of America by Cherry Lake Publishing Group
Ann Arbor, Michigan
www.cherrylakepublishing.com

Reading Adviser: Beth Walker Gambro, MS, Ed., Reading Consultant, Yorkville, IL
Content Adviser: Kelisa Wing
Book Design and Cover Art: Felicia Macheske

Photo Credits: © John Warner/Shutterstock, 5; Library of Congress/Photo by Gordon Parks, LOC Control No.: 2017843166, 7; Library of Congress/Photo by Marion Post Wolcott, LOC Control No.: 2017754826, 9; Library of Congress/Photo by Esther Bubley, LOC Control No.: 2017862148, 10; Schomburg Center for Research in Black Culture, The New York Public Library. (1937, 1940, 1941, 1951, 1952, 1953, 1956, 1961). The Negro Travelers' Green Book: Retrieved from https://digitalcollections.nypl.org, 13; Library of Congress/Artwork by George Edward Madeley, LOC Control No.: 2014649335, 15; © Naeblys/Shutterstock, 17; Library of Congress/Photographer unknown, LOC Control No.: 2016840297, 19; Library of Congress/Photo by American Red Cross, LOC Control No.: 2017679766, 21; Library of Congress/Photo by Dick Demarsico, LOC Control No.: 2006689554, 22; Library of Congress/Photo by Warren K. Leffler, LOC Control No.: 2003688162, 25; © Rommel Canlas/Shutterstock, 28; © Sheila Fitzgerald/Shutterstock, 30

Graphics Throughout: © debra hughes/Shutterstock.com; © Natewimon Nantiwat/Shutterstock.com

Library of Congress Cataloging-in-Publication Data

Names: Winn, Kevin P., author. | Wing, Kelisa, author.
Title: Jim Crow and policing / written by Kevin P. Winn, Kelisa Wing.
Description: Ann Arbor, Michigan : Cherry Lake Publishing, [2022] | Series: Racial justice in America: histories | Includes index. | Audience: Grades 4-6 | Summary: "The Racial Justice in America: Histories series explores moments and eras in America's history that have been ignored or misrepresented in education due to racial bias. Jim Crow and Policing explores the unjust laws and law enforcement policies Black people have faced in a comprehensive, honest, and age-appropriate way. Developed in conjunction with educator, advocate, and author Kelisa Wing to reach children of all races and encourage them to approach our history with open eyes and minds. Books include 21st Century Skills and content, as well as activities created by Wing. Also includes a table of contents, glossary, index, author biography, sidebars, educational matter, and activities"— Provided by publisher.
Identifiers: LCCN 2021010773 (print) | LCCN 2021010774 (ebook) | ISBN 9781534187474 (hardcover) | ISBN 9781534188877 (paperback) | ISBN 9781534190276 (pdf) | ISBN 9781534191679 (ebook)
Subjects: LCSH: African Americans—Segregation—History—Juvenile literature. | African Americans—Legal status, laws, etc.—History. | African Americans—History—1877-1964—Juvenile literature. | United States—Race relations—Juvenile literature. | Racism—United State—History—Juvenile literature.
Classification: LCC E185.61 .W766 2022 (print) | LCC E185.61 (ebook) | DDC 323.1196/073—dc23
LC record available at https://lccn.loc.gov/2021010773
LC ebook record available at https://lccn.loc.gov/2021010774

Cherry Lake Publishing Group would like to acknowledge the work of the Partnership for 21st Century Learning, a Network of Battelle for Kids. Please visit http://www.battelleforkids.org/networks/p21 for more information.

Printed in the United States of America
Corporate Graphics

Kevin P. Winn is a children's book writer and researcher. He focuses on issues of racial justice and educational equity in his work. In 2020, Kevin earned his doctorate in Educational Policy and Evaluation from Arizona State University.

Kelisa Wing honorably served in the U.S. Army and has been an educator for 14 years. She is the author of *Promises and Possibilities: Dismantling the School to Prison Pipeline*, *If I Could: Lessons for Navigating an Unjust World*, and *Weeds & Seeds: How to Stay Positive in the Midst of Life's Storms*. She speaks both nationally and internationally about discipline reform, equity, and student engagement. Kelisa lives in Northern Virginia with her husband and two children.

CHAPTER 1

What Was Jim Crow Segregation?

The United States has a long history of racism and inequality. Many groups of people have been targeted, but Black people have a unique history of experiencing racism in this country. This is because of the history of slavery. During slavery, White Europeans and Americans captured Africans and forcefully brought them to the United States. Even after slavery was outlawed, Black people continued to be treated unfairly.

One form of this unfair treatment was legal. It was called Jim Crow segregation. Under this system of racism, Black people had fewer rights than White people. Although it was the most extreme in the South, it appeared all over the country.

Jim Crow laws were in place from 1877 through the 1960s. They began after the Civil War. Southern White people didn't think enslaved Black people should be free. They definitely didn't want Black people to advance in society. According to them, Black people were not equal to White people.

Much of the unfair treatment of Black people in America today can be traced back to the Jim Crow laws.

But where did the name Jim Crow come from? It started in 1928 with a racist actor. His name was Thomas Rice. As a White man, he performed in minstrel shows wearing blackface. It was very offensive. The character he played was named Jim Crow. Through his portrayal, Rice made fun of Black people. He played into stereotypes. His show became very popular. The name Jim Crow soon became an offensive name for Black people. Many White people liked the insulting name. It stuck.

The South lost the Civil War in 1865. After this, a period called Reconstruction began. It lasted until 1877. During Reconstruction, the U.S. government tried to rebuild the South. Black people gained more rights. White people didn't like this. In response, they enacted Black codes. These rules tried to stop Black people from moving up in society. These codes were the beginnings of the official Jim Crow segregation.

After Reconstruction, the U.S. government made it clear that it was okay to treat Black people as inferior. It became especially obvious in 1896 during a U.S. Supreme Court case called *Plessy v. Ferguson*. Homer Plessy, a biracial man from Louisiana, didn't think it was right that Black people should have to sit in a separate train car.

He sat in a Whites-only car. A detective arrested him. Plessy challenged his arrest in court and lost. The Supreme Court ruled that "separate but equal" was legal. This ruling opened the door to widespread segregation throughout the country.

In the 1800s, much of America was segregated, including train cars.

CHAPTER 2

Life Under Jim Crow Segregation

In former slaveholding states, Black people couldn't escape segregation. The system was complete. There were signs posted in public places indicating the separation. For example, White people and Black people had to use different entrances into buildings. They needed to wait in separate areas of bus and train stations. They couldn't drink from the same water fountains. If Black people broke these rules, they would be punished. Not gently, either. Black people could be arrested and imprisoned by law. Often, White people attacked them in racial terror lynchings.

Black people often had to use a separate entrance for movie theaters and other places of business.

Jim Crow segregation wasn't just written into law. It was a way of life. Black people couldn't marry White people. Black men couldn't look White women in the eyes without the fear of being lynched.

It was also a part of etiquette and daily activities. When speaking to a White person, a Black person needed to address them with their proper title, such as "Mr." or "Mrs." However, White people didn't address Black people the same way. They used only their first names. It was their way of telling Black people that they didn't deserve a title—that they were unequal. White and Black people couldn't have fun together, either. In fact, a 1930 law in Birmingham, Alabama, specifically said that Black people and White people playing dominos and checkers together was illegal.

Segregation in public transportation was a major issue throughout Jim Crow. Black people challenged it many times. During Freedom Rides, Black and White **activists** sat together on public buses. This protest helped bring about the downfall of Jim Crow segregation during the civil rights movement. The Freedom Rides were a form of the civil disobedience and non-violent resistance that defined the civil rights movement.

White people worked hard to restrict the freedoms of Black people. They watched Black people's every move. In fact, Black people couldn't travel around the country like White people could. Hotels wouldn't let them spend the night. Restaurants wouldn't serve them food, and gas stations wouldn't allow Black people to fill up their cars. Black travelers had to pack extra cans of gas on trips in case they ran out and couldn't find a Black-friendly gas station.

Black people resisted this unfair treatment. They were creative. A mailman, Victor Hugo Green, came up with an idea called the *Green Book*. It was a guide to all the places around the country that served Black people. Victor Hugo Green knew he couldn't travel around the country and review each of the places in his book himself. He got help from other Black mailmen. They scouted out different places on their routes that were friendly to Black customers and reported back to Green. It was an effective way for Black travelers to find places to spend the night or just have access to basic human necessities like toilets. The *Green Book* was published from 1936 to 1966.

The *Green Book* was essential for Black people and families traveling in the United States in the mid-1900s.

When people think of Jim Crow, they often only think of the South. People normally don't think about the North as being unjust, but it was. Although there were not as many obvious or official forms of segregation, Jim Crow existed in the Northeast, Midwest, and West. Black people couldn't live in the same neighborhoods as White people. For example, White people used restrictive covenants in their neighborhoods. This meant that only White people could buy houses in certain neighborhoods. Not only that, but the house deed said that they could never sell their houses to Black people. These practices contribute to continued segregation in the United States today.

Sundown towns were located throughout the Northeast, Midwest, and West. In these towns, if a Black person was outside after the sun went down, they could be attacked and arrested.

The racist "Jim Crow" character created by Thomas Rice

Apartheid in South Africa

From 1948 to 1994, South Africa had a system called apartheid. It divided its citizens into three categories: Whites, Coloureds, and Africans. "Coloureds" referred to people of any non-White, non-African descent or of mixed race. Similar to Jim Crow segregation, laws were passed to restrict the country's African and Coloured population. People were required to carry passes. This identified which group they belonged to and which areas of cities they could enter. Families that identified as interracial were forced to split up under these cruel laws.

One of the most devastating actions was the forced removal of people from their homes. From the 1950s to the 1980s, millions of people were relocated. Perhaps the most notable forced relocation took place in 1955. It happened in a neighborhood called Sophiatown in Johannesburg—one of the world's biggest cities—where 50,000 Black people lived. Without much warning, armed police entered Sophiatown. They loaded everyone's belongings on trucks and forced them to move into a new area, called Soweto. Sophiatown was bulldozed and the buildings destroyed. The neighborhood was rebuilt as a suburb for White people called Triomf.

FOR USE BY WHITE PERSONS

THESE PUBLIC PREMISES AND THE AMENITIES THEREOF HAVE BEEN RESERVED FOR THE EXCLUSIVE USE OF WHITE PERSONS.

By Order Provincial Secretary

VIR GEBRUIK DEUR BLANKES

HIERDIE OPENBARE PERSEEL EN DIE GERIEWE DAARVAN IS VIR DIE UITSLUITLIKE GEBRUIK VAN BLANKES AANGEWYS.

Op Las Provinsiale Sekretaris

Segregation and unjust laws to support it have been a problem all over the world.

CHAPTER 3

Jim Crow and Policing

As Jim Crow segregation grew, so did modern policing. Although policing in the United States was originally used to keep the peace, it morphed into controlling Black people. This form of policing began during slavery. White people created slave patrols to capture and punish escaped enslaved people. They used force and torture to punish the Black people that they caught.

After Reconstruction ended in 1877, the police enforced Jim Crow segregation laws. They stopped Black people on the streets and arrested them, even when they had done nothing wrong. In the South, many policemen were part of the Ku Klux Klan (KKK). This White terrorist group believes in White supremacy. The KKK, which remains alive and active today, regularly lynched Black people for breaking laws such as "looking at a White woman" or "not stepping aside on the sidewalk to allow a White person to pass."

The KKK was full of White people who worked in government, law enforcement, or as local business owners.

The United States has experienced many racist riots and massacres throughout its history. Many of them happened throughout the 20th century, and they continue today. Deadly racist violence occurred in Chicago, Illinois, in 1919. Three years later, a report that studied the reasons for the riots was released. It said that the police targeted Black people. It reported that Black people faced harsher charges for crimes than White men who had done the same thing.

In Oklahoma during the 1921 Tulsa Race Massacre, White police officers **deputized** White citizens. This meant that White police officers gave White mobs guns and allowed them to use force against and murder innocent Black people.

The 1921 riot in Tulsa destroyed the Black community there.

Police violence against Black communities has been a problem since the police force originated in 1844.

After racist violence in the Harlem neighborhood of New York City in the 1930s, another report was released. It said almost the same thing that the Chicago report said—police needed more accountability for the way they treated Black people.

More reports from other cities came out in 1943 and 1968. They all said the same thing, yet the violence against Black people continues today.

Today, Black people continue to be arrested at higher rates than White people. Black people only make up 13 percent of the U.S. population. In 2019, they made up more than 30 percent of all of arrests and 23.4 percent of victims of all fatal police shootings. Further, Black people are more likely to die in police custody than any other racial group.

CHAPTER 4

Jim Crow Is Still Alive Today

Official Jim Crow segregation laws ended in the 1960s because of the civil rights movement. Black people and White people who didn't think Jim Crow was fair fought for human rights for Black people. The work that activists did contributed to the Civil Rights Act in 1964. This act was passed by the U.S. Congress and signed by President Lyndon B. Johnson. It made segregated schools illegal. It outlawed job discrimination against Black people and ended voting restrictions.

The civil rights movement had supporters of all races from across
the country, but there were others who did not want to see those
laws signed.

Although Jim Crow laws are illegal, their legacy remains. Black people remain subjugated in this country in several ways. Some White people have found loopholes in the laws so that Black people and other people of color remain segregated. One important and growing problem is mass incarceration.

Mass incarceration refers to the huge number of people in the prison system. This doesn't just mean people who are in prisons and jails. This problem continues even when someone is freed from jail or prison. They remain in the criminal justice system, as the consequences of crimes stick to people long after they leave prison. Black people have especially been targeted by this country's justice system.

The United States has the highest rate of imprisoning its people in the world. In fact, of all imprisoned people on Earth, the United States has one-fifth of them.

The Thirteenth Amendment abolished slavery. This was huge, but the language in the amendment is tricky. It states, "Neither slavery nor involuntary servitude, except as a punishment for crime whereof the party shall have been duly convicted, shall exist within the United States, or any place subject to their jurisdiction." Look at the words *except as a punishment for crime*. What does that actually mean?

Many scholars believe this wording has been used against Black people. Once again, their movements are restricted. If a Black person is accused of a crime, by law, they can be punished through slavery and involuntary servitude. Through this sneaky wording, Jim Crow remains alive and active. Black people have higher incarceration rates than any other group in the United States. They often receive worse punishments than White people who commit the same crime. There are so many people in the prison system that innocent Black people remain incarcerated for long periods of time. This is because the prison system cannot handle all of the paperwork to free innocent people quickly.

In Alabama, one-third of all Black men have been imprisoned.

Modern policing continues Jim Crow segregation. The enormous presence of officers and surveillance in inner city neighborhoods polices even those who have done nothing wrong. When Black people are imprisoned, their movements are restricted. Because there isn't enough room in prisons and jails, a new system of e-carceration has begun. It means that people in the prison system can live at home, but they must wear a tracking device. They only can go a certain distance. Huge percentages of people in certain communities are now being watched, unable to leave their neighborhoods.

In May 2020, a police officer in Minnesota murdered a man named George Floyd. Three other police officers stood by and watched. All four men were charged with responsibility for the murder. The murder was filmed. People all over the world saw the cruelty of police against Black people. The video sparked protests around the world. Protesters called for more police accountability. Efforts continue to seek justice for George Floyd and other victims of police brutality against Black people.

During the summer of 2020, there were protests against police brutality in more than 60 countries around the world.

SHOW WHAT YOU KNOW

Do you know what the school-to-prison pipeline is? The school-to-prison pipeline describes a system where Black and Hispanic/Latinx students are more harshly punished in school than White students. They are actually three to four times more likely to be punished in school for the same offenses than White students are. This leads to BIPOC—Black, Indigenous, and people of color—students being referred to the juvenile justice system. These students then have a greater chance of entering the criminal justice system. It is another form of policing and injustice for Black people.

We can stop the school-to-prison-pipeline by working with teachers to make class rules that are fair for everyone. For this show what you know assignment, find out what your classroom rules are. Ask your teacher if he/she might consider allowing students to help with the rules. Share how you think making rules as a whole class can help stop the school-to-prison pipeline.

Do you know there are so many different ways to show what you know? Rather than using traditional ways to display knowledge, try something new to complete this assignment. Here are some ideas:

1. Rap
2. Mural
3. Musical
4. Debate
5. Web page
6. Speech
7. Bulletin board
8. Jigsaw puzzle
9. Show and tell
10. Essay
11. Diorama
12. Performance
13. Podcast
14. Journal
15. OR add your own...

EXTEND YOUR LEARNING

Wing, Kelisa J. *Promises and Possibilities: Dismantling the School-to-Prison Pipeline*. New York, NY: CreateSpace Independent Publishing Platform, 2018.

GLOSSARY

accountability (uh-kown-tuh-BIH-luh-tee) holding someone responsible for something

activists (AK-tih-vists) people who work for a cause

apartheid (uh-PAHR-tyt) a system of laws in South Africa that separated people of different races

blackface (BLAK-fayss) wearing dark makeup, usually by a White person, to impersonate a Black person

deputized (deh-PYOO-tyzed) specific powers given to someone for a little while

fatal (FAY-tuhl) leading to death

incarceration (in-kahr-suh-RAY-shuhn) being put in jail or prison

legacy (LEG-uh-see) long-term effects

mass incarceration (MASS in-kahr-suh-RAY-shuhn) the process by which the United States imprisons its people at high rates

minstrel shows (MIN-struhl) offensive performances by White people that make fun of Black people

offensive (uh-FEN-siv) something that is mean or rude

racial terror lynchings (RAY-shuhl TER-uhr LINCH-ings) violent attacks by white people on BIPOC, especially Black people, to scare and control them; usually done through torture, murder, and hanging

Reconstruction (ree-kuhn-STRUK-shuhn) period after the Civil War when Southern states were rebuilding and Black people had more rights

restrictions (ri-STRIK-shuhns) not being allowed to do something

restrictive covenants (ri-STRIK-tiv KUH-vuh-nuhnts) agreements that didn't allow White people to sell houses to Black people in White neighborhoods

stereotypes (STER-ee-oh-types) simplified beliefs about a group of people

subjugated (SUHB-jih-gay-tuhd) ruled over

White supremacy (WITE suh-PREH-muh-see) the incorrect belief that White people and their ideas are superior to all others

INDEX